*Blue Bell Hill   Games*

# Blue Bell Hill Games

Compiled by
R. A. Smith

Head Teacher,
Blue Bell Hill Junior School,
Nottingham

Illustrated by
David McKee

Kestrel Books

Kestrel Books
Published by Penguin Books Ltd
Harmondsworth, Middlesex, England

Copyright © 1982 by Nottinghamshire County Council
Illustrations Copyright © 1982 by David McKee

All rights reserved. No part of this publication may be reproduced, stored in a retrieval system, or transmitted in any form or by any means, electronic, mechanical, photocopying, recording, or otherwise, without the prior permission of the Copyright owner.

First published in 1982

ISBN 0 7226 5726 9

Composition in Photina by
Filmtype Services Limited
Scarborough, North Yorkshire

Printed in Great Britain by
Butler & Tanner Ltd
Frome and London

## Contents

1. Skipping Games    7
2. Two-Ball    27
3. Dancing and Singing    37
4. Clapping Games    47
5. Counting-out Rhymes    57
6. Other Games    67

# 1 · Skipping Games

*All these games are played with two people turning the rope, one at each end, others running in over the rope to skip in turn*

## FORTUNE TELLING RHYMES

### Ada Apple, Lemon Tart

*One skips while others turn and sing the rope*

◀ Ada apple, lemon tart,

Tell me the name of your sweetheart

*Chant alphabet until skipper misses a step and stops rope; she then gives name of boy beginning with letter just called out*

A B C D E F G, etc.

What will you get married in?

*Repeat last line until skipper again misses and stops rope*

◀ Rags, silver, satin.

How many children will you have?

*Count until skipper stops rope again. Her 'fortune telling' is now complete*

◀ 1 2 3 4 5, etc.

8 · SKIPPING GAMES

## On the Mountain

*All chant and turn rope while one child skips*

◀ On the mountain stands a lady
Who she is I do not know
All she wants is gold and silver
All she wants is a nice young man.

*Chant alphabet until skipper misses a step and stops rope; she then gives name of boy beginning with letter just called out*

◀ A B C D E F G, etc.

Where will you marry?

*Repeat last line until skipper misses and stops rope*

◀ Registry office, church or chapel?

Where will you live?

*Repeat last line until skipper stops rope*

◀ Mansion, cottage or pigsty?

How many children will you have?

*Keep counting until skipper stops rope*

◀ 1 2 3 4 5, etc.

SKIPPING GAMES · 9

## I Know a Little Boy

(the rest is chanted)

*One skips while everyone sings or chants*   ◀ I know a little boy and he is double-jointed

Gave me a kiss and made me disappointed

Gave me another to match the other.

How many kisses did he give me?

*Count until skipper stops rope*   ◀ 1  2  3  4, etc.

Took me down the river side

And sat me on his knee

And said 'Me Ducky Darling

Will you Marry Me?'

*Repeat until skipper stops rope*   ◀ Yes, No, Yes, No, etc.

How many children will you have?

*Count until skipper misses and stops rope*   ◀ 1  2  3  4, etc.

*When skipper stops, last colour called is that of her children*

◄ What colour will they be?

Black, white, black, white, etc.

Where will they live?

*Repeat last line until rope is stopped by skipper*

◄ Pigsty, palace, house.

What colour will you get married in?

*Repeat last line until rope is stopped*

◄ Gold, white, silver.

What material?

*Again repeat last line until rope is stopped*

◄ Silk, satin, rags.

Is it true or is it false?

*Repeat last line until rope is stopped*

◄ True, false.

Will you be out, or will you not?

*Repeat until rope is missed or stopped by skipper. If the rope is stopped on 'NO', skipper has another turn*

◄ Yes, No, Yes, No, etc.

SKIPPING GAMES · 11

ACTION RHYMES

*In all these rhymes two people turn rope, and one person runs in and does actions while skipping*

## Cowboy Joe from Mexico

One person runs in and starts skipping ◀ Cowboy Joe from Mexico

Skipper pretends to ride a pony ◀ Riding on a pony-O,

Hands in the air ◀ Hands up, stick 'em up

Touch ground ◀ Drop your guns and pick them up

Skipper runs out ◀ And off you go.

## Banana Splits

One person runs in ◀ Banana splits, banana splits,

Jump from side to side ◀ Wibble wobble, wibble wobble,

Run out ◀ Banana splits.

Another version is:

Jelly on the plate, jelly on the plate,
Wibble wobble, etc.

SKIPPING GAMES · 13

# Charlie Chaplin Went to France

*One person skips while others turn rope and chant*

◄ Charlie Chaplin went to France
To teach the ladies how to dance,

*Skipper turns round on the spot, touching heel and toe alternately to the ground*

◄ Heel, toe, round we go,

Don't forget the double O

*The rope is turned faster and faster. If the skipper stops the rope before 10 is reached they are out, otherwise they have another turn*

◄ 1 2 3 4 5 6 7 8 9 10.

14 · SKIPPING GAMES

## High, Low, Medium, Slow

Person skips till she fouls the rope. The word at which the skipper stops determines how she skips for the rest of her turn. For 'dolly', she holds her body stiffly while skipping, for 'rocker', rope is rocked, for 'pepper', rope is turned very fast, for 'low', skipper crouches

◀ High, low, medium, slow,

Dolly, rocker, pepper, low.

SKIPPING GAMES · 15

*Eva Weaver, Chimney Sweeper*

*Rhyme chanted once while rope is swung from side to side and skipper jumps over it*

◀ Eva Weaver, chimney sweeper,

Bought a wife and could not keep her,

Bought another to match the other,

*Rhyme chanted second time while rope is turned normally*

◀ Please turn me over.

*Rhyme chanted third time while rope is turned faster and faster until skipper is out*

16 · SKIPPING GAMES

## Jump Mississippi

*This game can be played either with a different child running in and out for each verse or one child doing all four verses before the next one has a turn*

*Ordinary skipping*

◀ Jump Mississippi,

If you miss a loop you're out.

*Hopping on one foot*

◀ Hop Mississippi,

If you miss a loop, etc.

*Jump up in the air while the rope goes under, with legs split from knees down*

◀ Scissors Mississippi, etc.

*Cover one eye while skipping*

◀ One eye Mississippi, etc.

SKIPPING GAMES · 17

## 1, 2, 3, on to Lulu

*One skips normally until the words 'on to Lulu' are chanted – skipper touches ground while rope is raised and turned over head*

◀ 1, 2, 3, on to Lulu,

4, 5, 6, on to Lulu,

7, 8, 9, on to Lulu,

10, on to Lulu, start again.

18 · SKIPPING GAMES

## Pick a Penny up

*Skipper has to touch ground every time the words 'pick a penny up' are said*

◄ Pick a penny up, pick a penny up;

Pick a penny

Pick a penny

Pick a penny up.

SKIPPING GAMES · 19

## Not Last Night but the Night Before

Not last night but the night before,

24 robbers came knocking at the door.

As I went down to let them in,

*At last line skipper turns around on the spot* ◀ One says Spanish lady, turn around,

*Skipper touches ground* ◀ Spanish lady touch the ground,

*Kicks one leg in the air* ◀ Spanish lady do the kicks,

*Jumps in the air doing the splits* ◀ Spanish lady do the splits

*Skipper runs out* ◀ And out you go.

20 · SKIPPING GAMES

## When I Was in the Kitchen

*Skip with the rope*  ◀ When I was in the kitchen,

*Mime sewing*  ◀ Doin' a bit of stitchin',

*Another person runs in to skip*  ◀ In came a burglar man

*Second person pushes first one out*  ◀ And pushed me out.

*A similar rhyme is:*

When I was in the garden,
Eating a banana,
In came a bogey man
And pushed me out.

SKIPPING GAMES · 21

## Dolly Dolly Climb the Stairs

*Running skip with knees lifted as if climbing stairs*  ◄ Dolly dolly climb the stairs,

*Puts hands together*  ◄ Dolly dolly say your prayers,

*Switches off light*  ◄ Dolly dolly switch off the light,

Dolly dolly spell goodnight:

*Rope is turned faster for last line*  ◄ G-O-O-D-N-I-G-H-T.

*A similar version in which the child performs actions at each line is:*

Teddy bear, teddy bear turn around,
Teddy bear, teddy bear touch the ground,
Teddy bear, teddy bear turn off the light,
Teddy bear, teddy bear say goodnight.

22 · SKIPPING GAMES

SIMPLE SEQUENCES

## *All In Together Girls*

All in together girls,

What a fine morning.

When I call your birthday,

You must jump in.

*All the months are called out in order and each player runs in when her birth month is called until everyone is skipping in the rope*  ◄  January, February, March, etc.

*Everyone runs out as birth month is called until rope is empty*  ◄  All out together girls,

What a fine morning, etc.

## *Cinderella Dressed in Red*

*One person skipping in the rope is Cinderella. As the hours are called, the rope is turned faster and faster until skipper stops the rope*

◄ Cinderella dressed in red

What time do you go to bed?

1 2 3 4 5 6 7 8 9 10 11 12.

## *Big Ben Strikes One*

*In each succeeding line, as the number progresses, the rope is turned faster and faster until the skipper stops the rope*

◄ Big Ben strikes one, tick, tock,

Big Ben strikes two, tick, tock,

Big Ben strikes three, tick, tock, etc.

## Up the Ladder

*Two people skip up and down the length of the rope while it is being turned, passing each other while the rhyme is chanted. If the count reaches 50 they have another go. If one of them stops the rope, they both take ends and turn the rope*

◀ Up the ladder, down the ladder,

Over the garden wall.

1  2  3  4  5, etc.

## Over the Stars

*Two turn the rope while everyone runs in, one after another, skipping over the rope for 'over the stars' and then running back underneath it for 'under the moon'*

◀ Over the stars

And under the moon.

SKIPPING GAMES · 25

## Rain, Rain Faster

The rope is turned while one or more run in to skip ◀ Rain, rain faster

Rope is turned very quickly ◀ Alley alley aster,

Rope is turned more slowly ◀ Rain, rain go away

Rope is turned as slowly as possible ◀ Come again another day.

## Salt, Vinegar, Mustard, Pepper

The rope is turned gradually faster and faster as the words are repeated until the skipper is out ◀ Salt, Vinegar, Mustard, Pepper.

# 2 · Two-Ball

*These rhymes are chanted or sung while throwing two balls against a wall*

## Ipsy Gypsy

Ipsy Gypsy lived in a tent,

Couldn't afford to pay the rent,

The rent man came the very next day

So Ipsy Gypsy ran away

Over the hills and far away

To where the gypsies used to play.

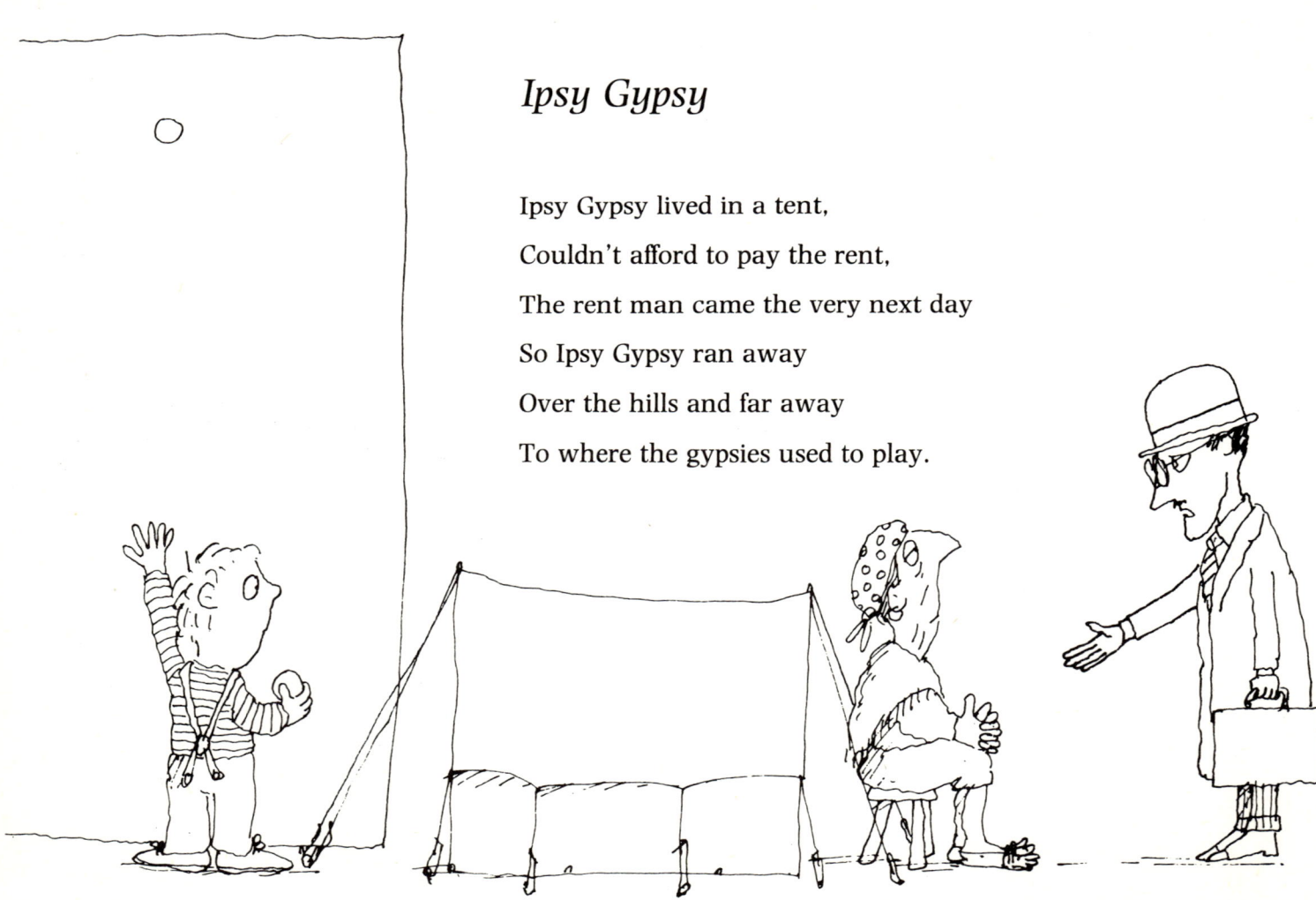

28 · TWO-BALL

## 2, 4, 6, 8

2, 4, 6, 8,
Mary sat at the cottage gate,
Eating cherries off a plate,
2, 4, 6, 8.

## Willy the Witch

Willy the witch fell in a ditch,
Upside down.

*These rhymes have special actions to go with the two-ball action*

## When I was One

*Pretend to eat something in between throwing balls*

◀ When I was one I ate a bun, ate a bun, ate a bun,
When I was one I ate a bun and that's the end of chapter one.

*Touch shoe while throwing balls*

◀ When I was two I buckled my shoe, buckled my shoe, buckled my shoe
When I was two I buckled my shoe and that's the end of chapter two.

*Touch knee while throwing balls*

◀ When I was three I grazed my knee, grazed my knee, grazed my knee, etc.

*Kick wall*

◀ When I was four I kicked the door, etc.

*Pretend to sit down*

◀ When I was five I sat on a hive, etc.

30 · TWO-BALL

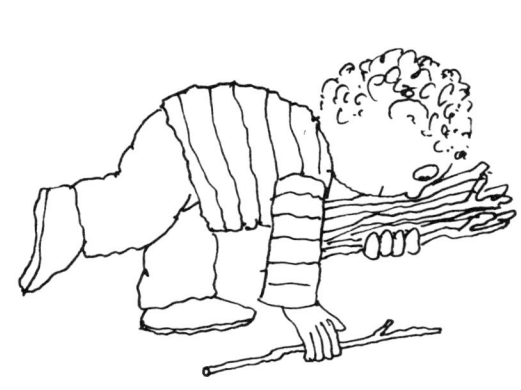

*Try to touch the ground*　　◀ When I was six I picked up sticks, etc.

*Jump up and down*　　◀ When I was seven I went to heaven, etc.

*Pretend to slam gate*　　◀ When I was eight I slammed the gate, etc.

*In between throwing balls put one hand in the air and pretend to swing*　　◀ When I was nine I swung on the line, etc.

*Try to mime this!*　　◀ When I was ten I sat on a hen, etc.

TWO-BALL · 31

*Here are two other rhymes which are similar and in which you make up your own actions to fit the words:*

When I was one I ate a bun,

Going to the seashore,

I jumped upon the pirate ship

And the captain said to me,

We're going this way, that way,

Sideways and backways,

Over the ocean wide,

A bottle of rum, to fill me tum,

And that's the end of chapter one.

*

One two, buckle my shoe,

Three four, knock at the door,

Five six, pick up sticks,

Seven eight, close the gate.

*And so on through the nursery rhyme to twenty*

## Oliver, Oliver, Oliver Twist

Oliver, Oliver, Oliver Twist

I bet you ten dollars you can't do this:

*Jump to a legs-apart position, and then bend knees* ◀ Stand at ease, bend your knees,

*March on the spot and turn around, still throwing balls* ◀ Do a quick march, under the arch,

*Bounce one ball on the ground* ◀ That's not all, drop the ball,

Oliver, Oliver, Oliver Twist.

## One, Two, Three Bollera

*In this rhyme the balls are thrown against the wall, and at the end of each line one ball is thrown from under one leg*

One, two, three bollera,

I saw sister Sarah

Sitting on an umberella

Eating jelly babies.

## Over the Garden Wall

*Turn around while throwing balls*  ◀ Over the garden wall

*Bounce a ball on the ground*  ◀ I let my baby fall

*Ordinary two-ball action*  ◀ My mother came out

*Ordinary two-ball action*  ◀ And gave me a clout,

*Turn around again*  ◀ Over the garden wall.

## Plainy Tim

Balls are thrown against the wall in ordinary underarm fashion

◀ Plainy Tim swallowed a pin

And that's the end of Plainy Tim.

Balls thrown overarm against the wall

◀ Over Tim swallowed a pin, etc.

Balls thrown against the wall, but to one side, so they do not bounce off the wall straight back to thrower

◀ Sidy Tim swallowed a pin, etc.

Balls thrown up to wall from under right leg

◀ 1st leg Tim swallowed a pin, etc.

Balls thrown from under left leg

◀ 2nd leg Tim swallowed a pin, etc.

Balls thrown with alternate underarm – overarm action

◀ Under over Tim swallowed a pin, etc.

TWO-BALL · 35

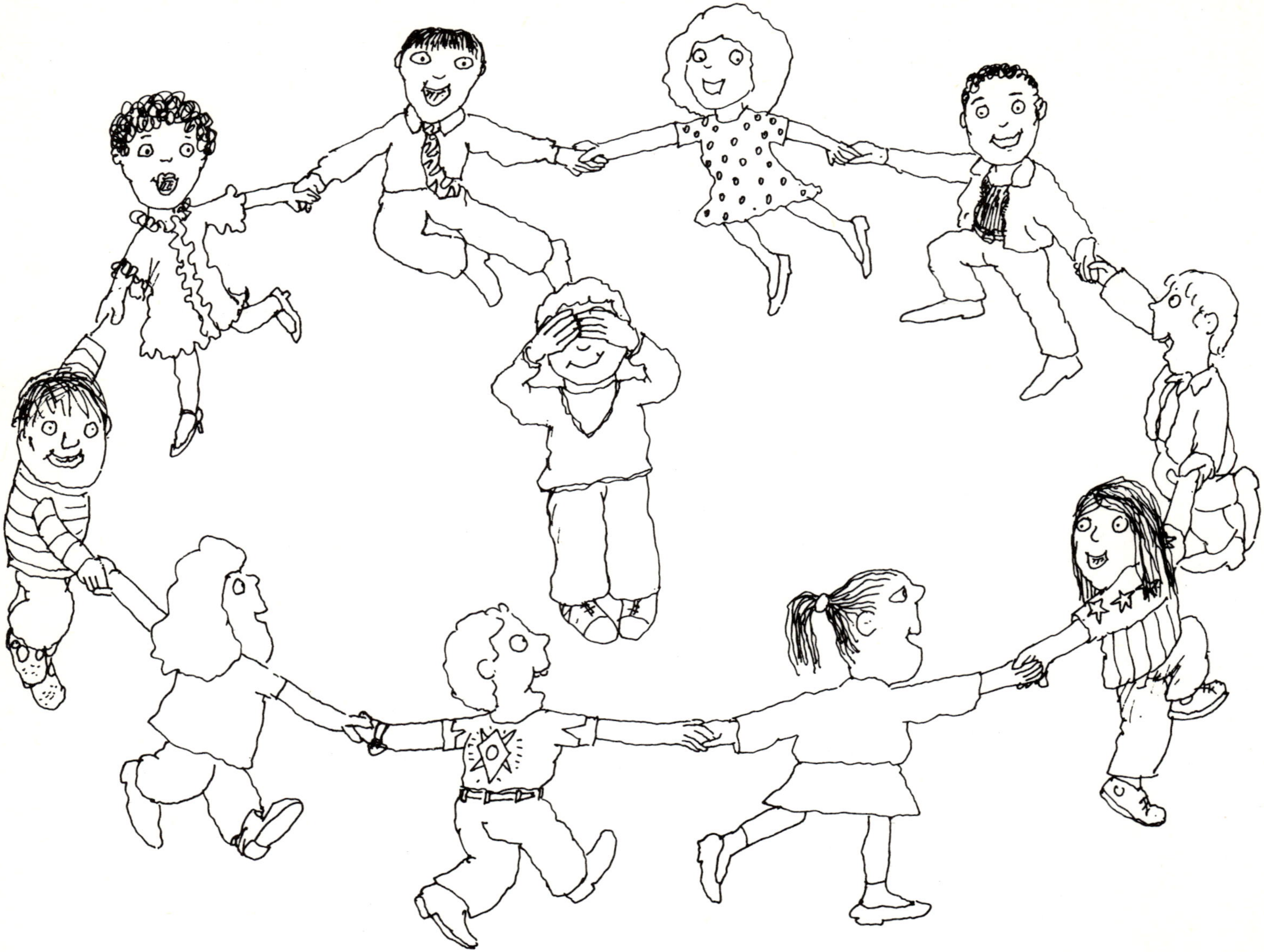

# 3 · Dancing and Singing

## I've Got a Daughter

Everyone in the game makes a circle, holding hands with one chosen person in the middle. Skip round and sing:

◄ I've got a daughter

Lives in New Yorker.

I'll do most anything

Circle runs in to bump person in the middle on 'OO'

◄ To keep her alive, OO!

She has a pair of legs

Just like two washing pegs:

For the following lines the circle stands still with arms folded while the person in the middle runs round the outside, chooses a player and pushes her into the circle on the last line to be the new person in the middle

◄ That's how the story goes.

Oolye, oolye, oolye-ay

Oolye-ay, oolye-ay,

Oolye, oolye, oolye-ay:

That is how the story goes.

38 · DANCING AND SINGING

## Wallflower

Make a circle with hands joined and walk round as you sing. One person is chosen to be named, but stays in her place in the circle

Wallflowers, wallflowers, growing so high;

We are little mermaids and we shall not die,

The chosen player's name is called ◀ All except for—

She's the only one

The players on either side of the named player shake her hands up and down with theirs ◀ So give her a shake, give her a shake

Turn her so that she now faces outwards in the circle. The rhyme is sung again and the next person to be named is one of those next to the first player. The game continues until everyone in the circle has been named and is facing outwards ◀ And turn her back to the wall again.

DANCING AND SINGING · 39

## Bluebird

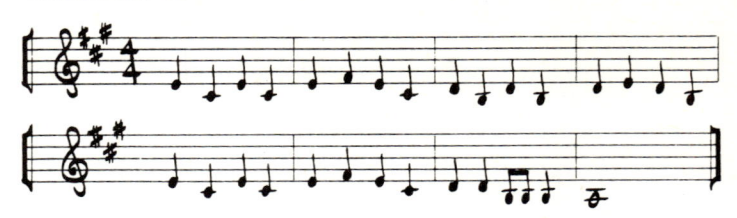

Everyone stands in a circle with hands joined high to make arches. One person is chosen to be a bluebird and in the first verse weaves in and out of the arches

On the last line the bluebird stops at the person she has arrived at, and pats her shoulders during verse 2

At the end of this verse the bluebird holds onto the waist of the second girl and they weave through the arches again while verse 1 is sung. The game continues with the line growing longer and longer until everyone is in it

Bluebird, bluebird through my window,

Bluebird, bluebird through my window,

Bluebird, bluebird through my window,

◄ Oh, my jolly and I.

Take a little girl and pat her on the shoulder,

◄ Take a little girl and pat her on the shoulder, etc.

40 · DANCING AND SINGING

## Susie Had a Baby

*All the players stand in a circle*

*Pretend to rock baby in arms*

*Pretend to lay baby in a bath*

*Motion with hands to show sinking and rising*

*Pretend to telephone*

*Take a step in with each line*

◀ Susie had a baby,
She called it Tiny Tim,

◀ She put it in the bath tub
To see if it could swim.

◀ It sank to the bottom,
It swam to the top,

◀ Susie phoned the doctor,
Susie phoned the nurse,
Susie phoned the lady with the alligator purse.

◀ In went the doctor,
In went the nurse,
In went the lady with the alligator purse.

DANCING AND SINGING · 41

*Point to face*

*Point to face looking amazed*

*Take a step out with each line*

*Clap hands twice*

◀ 'Measles,' said the doctor,

'Measles,' said the nurse,

◀ 'Chicken Spots,' said the lady with the alligator purse.

◀ OUT went the doctor,

OUT went the nurse,

OUT went the lady with the alligator purse.

◀ Bum, bum.

42 · DANCING AND SINGING

## I'm a Little Dutch Girl

A girl and a boy, or a girl pretending to be a boy, face each other. If more than two want to play, form two lines opposite each other

As they sing the first verse the girl goes forward to the boy and back. In the next verse the boy does the same

1. I'm a little Dutch girl, Dutch girl, Dutch girl, I'm a little Dutch girl, Tickerma, tackerma, teazer.

2. I'm a little Dutch boy, Dutch boy, Dutch boy, etc.

The girl goes forward and shows off an imaginary apron to the boy. In the next verse he shows off his trousers to the girl

3. Do you like my pretty apron, apron, apron? etc.

4. Do you like my baggy trousers, trousers, trousers? etc.

The girl holds out a necklace to the boy, who in the next verse comes forward and pretends to snatch it

5. Do you like my pretty necklace, necklace, necklace? etc.

6. Now I hate you, hate you, hate you, etc.

7. Now you've gone and broke it, broke it, broke it, etc.

The girl goes forward and back to the boy, as in verse 1. In the next verse it is the boy's turn

8. Do you forgive me, forgive me, forgive me? etc.

DANCING AND SINGING · 43

*The girl goes forward and back*

◄ 9. Yes I will forgive you, forgive you, forgive you, etc.

*The boy goes up to the girl as he asks her. In the next verse she goes up to him to give her answer*

◄ 10. Will you marry me, marry me, marry me? etc.

11. Yes I will marry you, marry you, marry you, etc.

*They both go forward and back to each other*

◄ 12. Now we're getting married, married, married, etc.

*They mime holding a baby*

◄ 13. Now we're having a baby, baby, baby, etc.

*They both go forward and back but they are bent over*

◄ 14. Now we're getting older, older, older, etc.

*Boy and girl put their hands in the air and jump up and down*

◄ 15. Now we're going to heaven, heaven, heaven, etc.

44 · DANCING AND SINGING

## Deep in the Forest

*Players sit on the ground either in a line or a circle. There are no actions for the first two lines*

Deep in the forest

Where nobody knows

*One hand on hip while the other makes a circle in the air* ◄ There's a boogy, boogy, boogy

*Rub fingers together to mime washing clothes* ◄ Washing her clothes

*The same action is done first to one side of the body and then the other* ◄ With a wish wash there,

And a wish wash here:

That's the way she washes her clothes.

*Repeat hand on hip and circling motion* ◄ And a boogy, boogy, boogy,

Boogy woo:

That's the way she washes her clothes.

DANCING AND SINGING

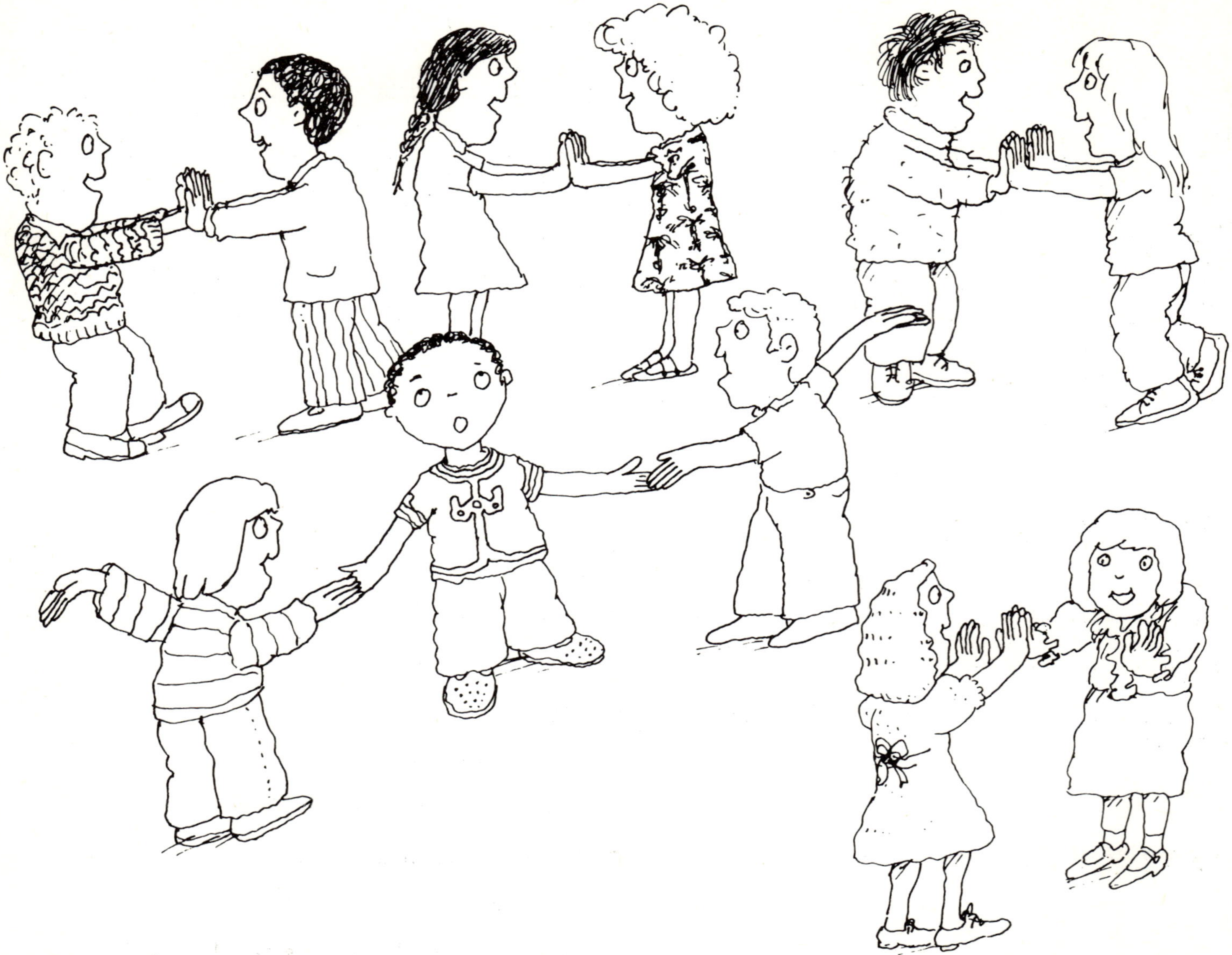

# 4 · Clapping Games

*These are more sophisticated versions of the basic 'Pat-a-cake' game. Most of these clapping games are played by two people opposite each other, or a group in a ring. When played in a ring, each player claps one hand of the person on either side of her*

*A basic repetition of clapping first both partners' hands and then own, until line 4, 'said, said, said', when both partners clap each other's hands three times. Works well played in a circle*

## I Went into a Baker's Shop

I went into a baker's shop

To buy a loaf of bread, bread, bread.

He wrapped it up in newspaper,

And this is what he said, said, said:

My name is I do I do,

Willy Wally Whiskers,

Chinese Chopsticks,

Merci.

## Down in the Jungle

*Clapping as in* Baker's Shop *until the last two lines when partners keep clapping both hands together*

Down in the jungle

Lives a big fat mamma

Who washes her clothes

With a bum, bum, bum,

Boogy, boogy boo.

CLAPPING GAMES · 49

## Popeye the Sailor Man

*Each syllable counts as a clapping beat, so actions are on:*

(1)  Hold hands out towards partner, left palm down and right palm up, and clap each other's hands
(2)  Clap hands with partner, hands up, palms out
(3)  Clap hands together
(4) and (5)  Repeat 1 and 2
(6) to (8)  Cross hands on chest: right hand, then left, then rest

*Clap as in line one*

*Repeat as in (1) (2) (3), (1) (2) (3), (1) and (2)*

*Repeat as in line one*

*Shake left hand, then right hand in the air, then both hands together for each 'dash'*

    1  2   3   4  5   6   7    8
Popeye the sailor man, full stop.

◄ Lives in a caravan, full stop.

When he goes swimming,

◄ He kisses all the women;

◄ Popeye the sailor man, full stop.

◄ Comma, comma, dash, dash.

50 · CLAPPING GAMES

## Under the Bam Bushes

*For each line follow instructions (1) (2) (3) for* Popeye the Sailor Man, *repeating with opposite hands*

*Clap hands with partner, three times*

*Repeat clapping actions of first two lines*

*Clap as before, but clap hands with partner for last two 'pom, poms'*

Under the bam bushes
Under the trees,
◀ Bum, bum, bum.
True love to you, my darling,
True love to me,
When we get married,
We'll raise a family:
◀ A boy for you, and a girl for me.
◀ Om tiddley om pom, pom, pom.

CLAPPING GAMES · 51

*As they sing, partners for each beat clap first their own hands, then right hand with partner's right, then own hands, then left hand with partner's left, etc., until 'puff puff', when both hands are clapped against partner's, twice*

## Om Pom Pay

Om pom pay, polonay polon eskee,

Om pom pay, polonay,

Acker dermit, so farnit,

Acker dermit, puff puff.

## A Sailor Went to Sea

*For each line clap own hands together, right hand with partner's right hand, own hands, left hand with partner's, then own hands together, but for 'sea, sea, sea' salute three times. Repeat for each line of verse*

1. A sailor went to sea, sea, sea,

    To see what he could see, see, see,

    And all that he could see, see, see,

    Was the bottom of the deep blue sea, sea, sea.

*Clapping as for verse 1, but make chopping action with right hand on left arm for 'chop, chop, chop'*

◀ 2. A sailor went to chop, chop, chop, etc.

*Same clapping, then tap own knees for 'knee, knee, knee'*

◀ 3. A sailor went to knee, knee, knee, etc.

*Same clapping, then tap chest, head (nut) and reach up (tree)*

◀ 4. A sailor went to chestnut tree, etc.

CLAPPING GAMES · 53

## Susie My Baby

*Forearms held out straight, hands down and swayed from side to side*

*Clap own hands, back of hands with partner, right hand with partner's right hand, own hands together, then left hand with partner, own hands together, and back of hands with partner. These clapping actions are repeated throughout the song until 'more, more, more' when partners clap both their hands together three times*

◀ Susie my baby

◀ I cannot play with you,

My Mummy's got the 'flu,

And German Measles too.

Slide down the rainbow,

And to my Jelly Tots.

Forever more, more, and more, more, more.

54 · CLAPPING GAMES

# 1,2,3, Together

*Two players, holding palms of hands together as if praying, brush backs of hands together against partner's, to left, right, and left. On 'together' each person claps own hands together*

◀ 1,2,3, together,

*Left hands point at partner while right hands clap together above left hands and then below*

◀ Up together, down together,

*With partner clap hands, back, front, touch knees with your own hands, then clap them together, slap sides with your own hands, then clap them together, bump hips, clap your hands*

◀ Back, front, knees together,

Sides together, bums together.

CLAPPING GAMES · 55

## Egg, Bacon, Cheese and Fat

*One person (A) is chosen to be 'on' or 'it'. The others stand with hands held out, palms up, and A taps each hand in turn to the rhyme*

Egg, bacon, cheese and fat,

Wedding cake, or wedding hat?

*The last person to be tapped is asked*

◀ Fast, slow, medium or a bit of everything?

*A then spins the person round according to their choice and then lets go of their hand. The player must stay in the position in which they land. This is done to each player in turn, the rhyme being repeated each time, and then, after the last one, A chooses a player and says*

◀ Wakey, wakey, rise and shine,

Make your bed,

And then make mine.

*The game then starts again*

56 · CLAPPING GAMES

# 5 · Counting-out Rhymes

*All the rhymes in this section are used to decide who will be 'on' (or 'it' or 'he') in the main game which is to follow. Usually those who want to take part in the game form a circle and one person recites a counting-out rhyme. By counting round the players in time to the words, one person is knocked out each time the rhyme is said until only one person is left.*
*Some rhymes are quite straightforward, others require a response from one of the players, and many have a standard last line using the word 'OUT'*

## Simple Counting-out Rhymes

Smack your chops,

Lick your lips,

Have a little bag

of *(pause)* chip sticks.

Eenie meenie mackeracker

Air I dominacker

Chickie packer alleracker

Om pom push.

And O-U-T spells out.

58 · COUNTING-OUT RHYMES

Eenie meenie miney mo
Catch a figure by the toe,
When it screams let it go,
Eenie meenie miney mo.
Like a dirty dishcloth inside OUT.

Cinderella, Cinderella,
Went to the ball,
Walked through the door,
Fell through the floor,
And OUT she went.

**COUNTING-OUT RHYMES**

Four white horses in a stable,

Pick one out and call it Mabel,

And O-U-T spells out.

One potato, two potatoes,

Three potatoes, four,

Five potatoes, six potatoes,

Seven potatoes, more.

One bad spud,

And O-U-T spells out.

Inky Pinky Ponky
Daddy had a donkey
Donkey died
Daddy cried
Inky Pinky Ponky.

John Wayne went to Spain
On a chocolate aeroplane,
Saw a ghost, eating toast,
Halfway up a lamp post,
And O-U-T spells out.

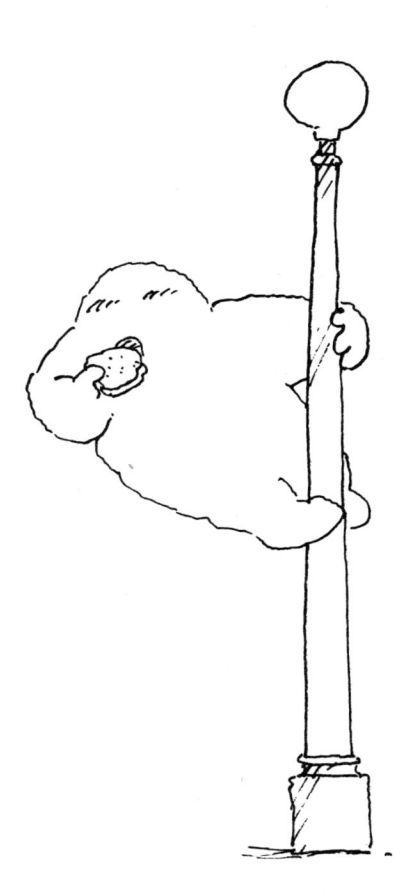

**COUNTING-OUT RHYMES · 61**

L-O-N-D-O-N spells London

And O-U-T spells out.

Sailing on the water like a cup and saucer,

And if you do not want to play

Pack your bags and go away,

For a week and a day,

And O-U-T spells out.

There's a fight on the hill,
Will you come, will you come?
Bring your own boxing gloves
And your own cream bun.
Slap it in the face,
Give them a box or two:
Box, box, box,
And knocked out are you.

*The following rhymes need an answer from one of the players in order to complete the count*

Dib, dib, dation, corporation,

How many buses are in the station?

*(e.g. Four)*

One, two, three, four

And O-U-T spells out.

Mrs Ink-Pink-Stink

Fell down the sink,

And how many miners did she hit?

*(e.g. Four)*

One, two, three, four

And O-U-T spells out.

Mickey Mouse built a house,

What colour was it?

*(e.g. red)*

R-E-D and O-U-T spells out.

There's a party on the hill,

Will you come, will you come?

Bring your own cup and saucer,

And your own cream bun.

'Can't afford it.'

Then tell me your boyfriend's name

*(e.g. John)*

He will be there, blowing kisses in the air,

And O-U-T spells out.

When did you last clean your Sunday Best Shoes?

*(e.g. Wednesday)*

Monday, Tuesday, Wednesday

And O-U-T spells out.

*This rhyme needs a ball and those in the circle should touch feet with their neighbour. It is often used to start the game Dobbie Ball (see Other Games section) by choosing a person with the rhyme*

*On the last word drop the ball and the person through whose legs the ball rolls is 'on' or 'it'*

Stir the rice, stir the rice,

Drop the sugar in.

# 6 · Other Games

*Use a counting-out rhyme to choose who is to be 'on' (or 'it' or 'he')*

*Players chant words, jumping alternately with left or right leg forward, and legs together. If at the end of the rhyme anyone does not have legs together they have a penalty, e.g. sock pushed down, coat off, lace untied. If subsequently that player finishes the rhyme with his legs crossed, the penalty is removed*

## Cat's Got the Measles

Cat's got the measles, the measles, the measles,

Cat's got the measles, and the measles got the cat.

68 · OTHER GAMES

## Letters in a Name

*Everyone stands in a line – the person 'on' stands a short distance away and calls out a letter. Players take one stride towards 'on' for every time that letter appears in their name. The first player to get to 'on' and home again, twice shouts 'Letters in a Name' and wins, becoming 'on'.*
*A variation is* Red Letter *in which one letter is chosen as a red letter. Whenever it is called, anyone making a move has to go back to the start*

OTHER GAMES · 69

## Sun and Moon

Two players are chosen to be Sun and Moon while the others bend over and make an arch. Sun must pass under the arches, but when she has been through an arch, that player can run off within agreed boundaries: Moon has to try and catch them. When Sun has passed under every arch Moon must then try and catch Sun. The game ends when everyone has been caught – the last person to be caught is Moon in the next game, the second to last is Sun

70 · OTHER GAMES

## Donkey

*Everyone in a line. First person throws a ball against the wall and jumps over it, the next in the line must catch it and then throw it against the wall to jump over themselves, and so on. If anyone misses a jump or doesn't catch the ball they are given the first letter D. The next time the same person makes a mistake, they add O, and the first person to collect the complete word Donkey is out*

OTHER GAMES

## Hop, Hop, Hop

Everyone stands with backs to the wall, except one chosen player, A, who taps each hand in turn, saying

◀ Hop, hop, hop,

To the lollipop shop,

And see how long it takes you.

Your mother says stop

Playing with boys

At this point A shouts to the other players to face the wall, taps one player, B, on the back and runs off. B quickly finishes the rhyme by shouting

◀ And you must stop right ...

There

and A must stand still. B hops round A and back to the wall again saying the rhyme. Then A and B stretch out to see if they can touch hands. If they can, they change places

*A similar game is*     # S-T-O-P

*Players face the wall, having chosen one person 'on' who taps one player and strides away for 8 long steps, saying*  ◀ S-T-O-P comma, comma, full stop.

*The player 'on' has tapped then has to hop 8 times towards him to the same words. If he can then reach across and touch 'on', the two change places*

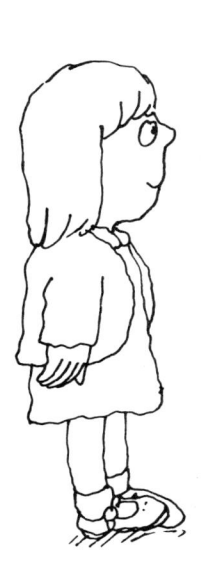

OTHER GAMES · 73

## Fruit and Veg

*One person is chosen 'on'. Two places are agreed to be fruit and veg. 'On' secretly decides on an object, the others guess if it is fruit or veg, and go to the place they have chosen. 'On' then calls out the object – those at the wrong place rush for the correct one. The last player is out. The last player left in the game is 'on' next time*

74 · OTHER GAMES

## Sly Fox

One person is chosen 'on' and stands a short distance away from the others who make a line. 'On' turns away from them, and they move nearer whenever they like. If 'on' turns and sees anyone moving they have to go back and start again. The first person to reach 'on' changes places

A similar game is

## Peep Behind the Curtain

'On' says

Peep behind the curtain, one, two, three

while the others move forward

OTHER GAMES · 75

## Catch

*One person is chosen 'on' and the rest stand in a line facing her as they chant*

*'On' shouts a colour. Anyone wearing that colour can cross safely, the others try to run past without getting caught. Anyone caught is 'on' next time*

Please Mr Fisherman,

May I cross the Chinese water,

On the way to Chinese school,

Eating Fish and Chips one day.

Players stand in a row against the wall. 'On' stands in front and calls out the name of a player, the action they are to do and how many times. If the player forgets to say May I they lose a turn. The first one to reach 'on' wins

## May I?

Strides – giant steps

Fairy steps – heel to toe

Umbrella – hand on the head and turn around a number of steps

Caterpillar – lie on the ground, move feet up then hands forward

Lamp post – stretch out on ground, then move feet to where fingertips touched.

OTHER GAMES · 77

## Port – Starboard

*All players go to port at start of game except for 'on' who gives instructions. When he calls 'Starboard' everyone runs there and the last player is out.
Other orders are:*

Scrub the deck – mime scrubbing on hands and knees

Clean the deck – touch something white

Captain's coming – salute with three fingers

Man in lifeboat – find a partner and jump on her back.    Any odd ones are out

Sharks – lie on stomach with feet up

Freeze – stop all action when this is called. If a further command is given without saying 'unfreeze' anyone obeying it is out.

## Streets

*Players divide into two teams, in opposing lines. The person chosen to be 'on' calls out commands*

Road – cross to opposing side and sit down

Street – cross and touch something white

Avenue – cross, turn round and sit down

Close – cross over.

*Last person to obey correctly or cross over, each time, is out. Game continues until one player is left, who is 'on' next time*

## Shake the Bed

*Two play as partners, holding hands which they shake up and down, chanting*

*When they call 'over' they lift their hands up and turn back to back, still holding hands. They repeat the rhyme and turn to the front again*

Shake the bed, shake the bed,

Turn the blankets over.

## Knockout

*One goalkeeper v. the rest. A certain number of goals are agreed, e.g. 3, the last player to score 3 is out. For the next round a different number of goals are agreed. Eventually only one player is left, who is the winner*

## Squash

*Two or more players with a ball. A goal is marked on the wall. The ball is thrown or kicked against the wall and on the rebound must be kicked first time to hit the goal, however far. If a small ball is used a tennis racquet is needed. Players start with 10 points and lose 1 point every time they fail to hit the goal*

## Tally-Ho, 1, 2, 3

*Two equal teams. 'A' team chooses a base, 'B' team runs off to hide within agreed boundaries while 'A' team count to 100. A team then set out to catch 'B' team and bring them to base, leaving one of their team to guard the base. The object is to catch the entire 'B' team – but those captured may be released by a team-mate who can reach the base and call 'Tally-Ho 1, 2, 3'. When all opposing team are caught, the teams change over*

# Princess

*A ball game. One player throws the ball to another, but thrower must call the catcher's name. If the catcher drops the ball she is out. The winner of the game becomes a Princess. If a Princess wins a subsequent game she becomes a Queen and overall winner. If a player throws a ball to a Princess and calls her by her name instead of her title, that player is out*

## Black Cat

At the beginning of the game each player has to catch hold of one of 'on's' fingers or thumbs except for the little finger. If there are 10 players then the little finger can be held. If more than 10 people play then 2 people have to be 'on'.
'On' tells any story mentioning coloured cats (e.g. an orange cat fell down a chimney and came through the door as a blue cat, etc.) until 'Black Cat' is mentioned. When this happens all the players run away and have to be 'dobbed'.
When dobbed, a player must go to a wall and put a hand on it. If a free player runs under the arm, the dobbed player is free. That is why 'on' must dob as many people as possible first

# T.V.

'On' chooses a TV channel, the time and the initial letters of the programme. The player who guesses the answer runs to one side and back again, becoming 'on' if correct

## Snakes

Two players, both 'on', hold either end of a rope. Between them they agree on two colours. Other players have to jump over the rope one at a time while it is shaken on the ground, calling out a colour as they do so. If this is one of the colours first chosen, that player becomes 'on' jointly, takes an end of the rope and chooses a colour

84 · OTHER GAMES

## Seize Her

Two people, A and B, are 'on'. They choose a subject, e.g. time. A whispers a time, e.g. two o'clock, to B. B then tells all the players that the subject is time and they call out the hours. Whoever says two o'clock is told by B to 'seize her' and she has to catch A before A can reach B. The player who catches A takes her place. If not, the original A stays with B but they reverse their roles

## Polo

'On' is at one side, the rest at the other. 'On' chooses a subject (e.g. houses, plants, etc.). If the subject is houses the others decide among themselves what sort of house each one is (e.g. flats, bungalow, detached, etc.). When 'on' shouts out 'flats' the player who had chosen flats runs towards the opposite side. 'On' does the same. The one who arrives at the opposite side first and shouts 'Polo' before the other is then 'on' and chooses a new subject

OTHER GAMES · 85

# Follow the Arrows

'On' has the chalk and the other players follow after an agreed count. 'On' draws arrows – these can be any combination of ↑ ↓ ← → ↖ or ✥ when the players would have to choose which direction to follow. The person who catches 'on' changes place, otherwise 'on' has another turn if home base is reached

# Hopscotch

1. ORDINARY

Any number plays, in turn, using the pitch marked out as in the diagram. Each player needs a stone or piece of slate, preferably a flattish shape. Player A throws her stone on to square 1, leaves it there and jumps through each square to 10 and back again – where two squares are adjacent (e.g. 2 and 3) she can land on two feet, one in each square, otherwise hop on one foot in a single square. When A has reached 10, and jumped back again, she stops at 2, picks up the stone from square 1 and jumps over square 1 to base. Next she throws the stone on to square 2, jumps over 1 on to 2, and repeats the procedure, but this time ends on square 3, picks up the stone from 2, and jumps over 2 on to 1 and back to base. The game is repeated until A has moved the stone through each square up to 10, and then back square by square to 1. If she misses or slips, the next player starts her turn, but A resumes play at her next turn, on the square she failed on before.

2. HOPSY

3. JUMPSY

When a player has successfully completed the game she selects a resting square and writes her initials on it – any other player stepping into this resting square is out. Then that player proceeds to play the whole game again, but doing Hopsy, that is hopping in each square on the same foot; on reaching the resting place, the player can put both feet down. Hopsy has to be played in reverse order, starting at 10, and working back to 1 and up to 10 again. A second resting square is chosen and the player moves on to Jumpsy, keeping both feet together all the time. Jumpsy is played from 1 to 10 and 10 to 1

# Marbles

This is a particularly unusual version. The game is played on a metal inspection cover. The two depressions are called charts, and the players try to get their marbles into these charts.

    One-er – one marble each
    Two-er – two marbles each, etc.

If a player gets a marble into a chart, he has another turn until he fails. The winner is the one who succeeds in sinking the final marble regardless of how many marbles he has got into the charts. Full charts are cleared out and guarded by a neutral onlooker

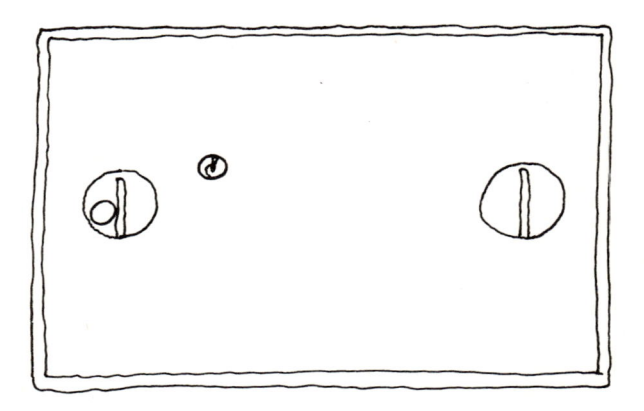

## 'DOBBIE' OR CATCHING GAMES

*All these are variations on the idea of one person being chosen to be 'on' (or 'he' or 'it') and trying to 'dob' or catch one of the other players so as to change places*

## Dobbie Ball

*The game is started with all the players in a circle with their legs apart and their feet touching each other's. On the last word of the rhyme*

Stir the rice, stir the rice,

Drop the sugar in

*the ball is dropped and the player through whose legs it rolls is 'on'. 'On' now has the ball and throws it at another player who in turn becomes 'on' if hit*

OTHER GAMES · 89

## Doctor Dobbie

*This is one of the funniest games to watch being played. The person caught has to keep touching the part of the body which has been 'dobbed'. Each player can be 'dobbed' more than once and can keep moving as long as possible while still touching the parts that are 'dobbed' – with hand, elbow, etc. When nobody can move any more the game begins again*

90 · OTHER GAMES

## Dobbie Little Men

'On' can only 'dob' a person who is upright – players are safe if they crouch, sit or lie down

## Dobbie Mud

A player who is caught has to stand with legs apart, and can only be freed by another player crawling through the legs, though 'on' tries to prevent this

OTHER GAMES · 91

# Dobbie Off-ground

'On' can only catch a player whose feet are on the ground

# Dobbie Scarecrow

A player who is caught has to stand like a scarecrow and can only be freed by another player running in under the outstretched arms, though 'on' naturally tries to prevent this

# British Bulldog

*Everyone on a line. 'On' stands a short distance away and calls out one name. That player has to get past 'on' to base without being caught. If caught, that player is 'on'. If the player succeeds in getting through then everyone has to get to base and the last caught is 'on' next time*

OTHER GAMES · 93